IN THE CITY

Carron Brown

Illustrated by Stef Murphy

Kane Miller
A DIVISION OF EDC PUBLISHING

A city is bustling with activity.

If you look closely at the buildings, parks, stores and theaters, you will spot lots of different things that happen in a city.

Shine a flashlight behind the page, or hold it up to the light to reveal the hidden sights of the city. Discover a world of great surprises.

Rise and Shine!
It's Monday morning
and people are getting
ready for the day.

Can you see a family
eating their breakfast?

Crunch! Munch!

This family lives at the edge of the city in an apartment. Other people live in apartments above and below this one.

To travel around the city, people walk, cycle, drive, or take the bus or train.

How many children are on the bus?

Off we go!

There are four children on
the bus so far. They are
on their way to school.

It's still early
morning and many people
are traveling to work.
Some people are already working.
Can you see them?

Here they are! These construction
workers started their day very early.
They are already busy building new
offices and homes in the city.

At the train station, people are catching trains or meeting visitors.

Can you see inside?

The whistle blows and a train pulls away.

A departure board shows people where each train is going.

Toot! Toot!

Many people in the city work in offices.

What happens in this one?

The people in this office are architects. They design new buildings, including skyscrapers.

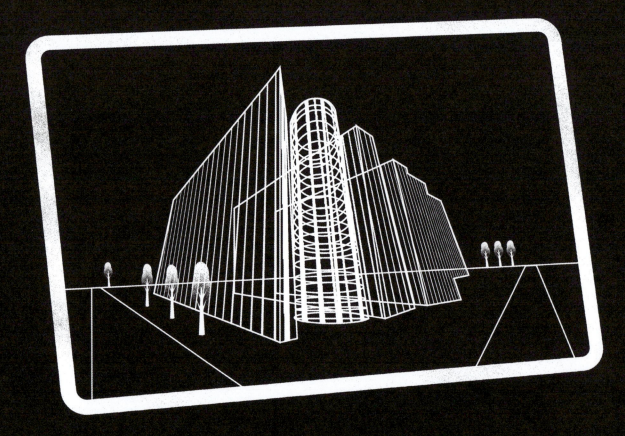

In the city, there are art
galleries and museums to visit.

What are
these
children
looking at?

It's a dinosaur skeleton.

The children are visiting
a natural history museum.
People go there to learn about
dinosaurs and the natural world.

ROAR!

The children have enjoyed
visiting the museum.

How will they
travel back to school?

Whoosh!

They will travel by subway.
Subway trains run in tunnels
under the city. The subway
stations are underground too.

Tourists take a boat
trip on the river.

What can they see
through the window?

They can see a huge building on
the riverside. This is where
the government makes important
decisions and new laws for the city.

Snap!
Snap!

This is a good place to take a picture.

At lunchtime, this park is full of people talking, walking and eating.

Is it really in the city?

Tweet! Tweet!

Yes! The park is in the center of
the city, surrounded by buildings.

There are many stores in the city. This department store sells all sorts of things. Each floor sells something different.

How do people get from one floor to another?

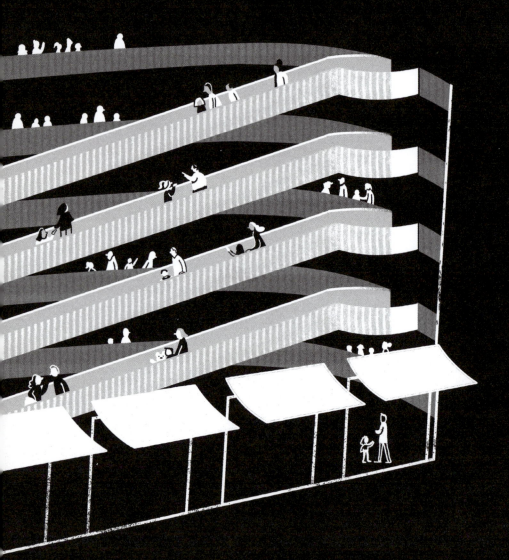

They ride on
escalators!

The escalators
can take them
from the ground
floor all the way up
to the top floor.

Planes fly to and
from the city
airport.

Can you see who
has just arrived?

Welcome!

Visitors come to the city on
vacation or to work. One plane can
carry hundreds of people.

At the theater, it's almost time for the show.
The lights are dimming, the music
is playing and everyone is excited.

Who's behind the curtain?

Ta-da!

The actors are dressed in wonderful costumes.

When the curtain opens,
they will begin the play.

People go to restaurants to eat
with family and friends.

Who is busy making
the meals?

The chefs in the kitchen
cook all kinds of different
food for people to eat.

Here comes dessert!
One of the servers is
bringing out a cake.
There must be something
to celebrate.

Chop!
Chop!

It's getting late, but some people are still at work.

Can you see someone behind the fountain?

Swish! Swish!

A street sweeper is keeping
the city clean.

People are going home to bed.

What does the city look like at night?

The city lights
glow and flash.

Many of the lights
will stay on all night.

The city is quiet now.
Most people are fast asleep.

But tomorrow when the sun rises,
the city streets will be filled with
busy people, noisy traffic and
chattering children.

Until then, good night!

There's more ...

There are all sorts of things to spot in the city.
See how many you can find the next time you are in a city.

Apartment Buildings Many people in cities live in apartment buildings. These buildings can have many stories, with staircases and elevators so that people can get to the top floors. An apartment might have a balcony instead of a backyard or a garden.

Trains Some trains travel around just one city, while others go from one town or city to another, or even to and from other countries. There are trains with restaurants, and sleeper trains have beds so passengers can sleep as the train travels through the night. Trains are made up of railroad cars joined together and they travel along a metal train track.

Motorbikes With just two wheels, motorbikes can move quickly around larger vehicles to beat traffic jams, and they're easy to park on the street. Drivers and riders wear crash helmets for safety.

Billboards Billboards are found all over the city. They are big signs that advertise different products—from clothes, books and food, to television shows, films and theater productions. Billboards are often placed near roads so that people can see them from their cars.

Planes Most cities have airports where planes can take off and land. There are small planes with propellers and huge planes with jet engines. People fly from all over the world to visit a city—it's faster than traveling by boat, train, bus or car.

Skyscrapers Skyscrapers are tall buildings that reach high up into the sky. They are used in crowded cities because they have lots of floors but do not take up much space on the ground. They often have offices inside and some of the tallest skyscrapers have more than 100 stories.